THE UNPROVOKED WAR

Russia's Invasion of
Ukraine

Craig E. Blohm

ReferencePoint
Press®

San Diego, CA

About the Author

Craig E. Blohm has written numerous books and magazine articles for young readers. He and his wife, Desiree, reside in Tinley Park, Illinois.

Picture Credits:
Cover: Drop Of Light/Shutterstock

4–5: Shutterstock
7: ZUMA Press, Inc./Alamy Stock Photo
11: Hum Images/Alamy Stock Photo
13: Sovfoto/UIG/Bridgeman Images
16: US State Department/Alamy Stock Photo
20: Maury Aaseng
23: UPI/Alamy Stock Photo

25: Reuters/Alamy Stock Photo
30: Sipa USA/Alamy Stock Photo
32: Sipa USA/Alamy Stock Photo
34: Ukrinform/Alamy Stock Photo
39: Reuters/Alamy Stock Photo
42: ZUMA Press, Inc./Alamy Stock Photo
45: Associated Press
50: Associated Press
52: Sipa USA/Alamy Stock Photo
55: Reuters/Alamy Stock Photo

LIBRARY OF CONGRESS CATALOGING-IN-PUBLICATION DATA

Names: Blohm, Craig E., 1948- author.
Title: The unprovoked war : Russia's invasion of Ukraine / by Craig E. Blohm.
Other titles: Russia's invasion of Ukraine
Description: San Diego, CA : ReferencePoint Press, 2023. | Includes bibliographical references and index.
Identifiers: LCCN 2022034592 (print) | LCCN 2022034593 (ebook) | ISBN 9781678204860 (library binding) | ISBN 9781678204877 (ebook)
Subjects: LCSH: Ukraine--History--Russian Invasion, 2022---Juvenile literature. | Russia (Federation)--Military policy--Juvenile literature. | Russia (Federation)--Foreign relations--Ukraine--Juvenile literature. | Ukraine--Foreign relations--Russia (Federation)--Juvenile literature.
Classification: LCC DK508.852 B56 2023 (print) | LCC DK508.852 (ebook) | DDC 947.7086--dc23/eng/20220719
LC record available at https://lccn.loc.gov/2022034592
LC ebook record available at https://lccn.loc.gov/2022034593

CONTENTS

IMPORTANT EVENTS IN RUSSIA'S WAR ON UKRAINE

March 1: A 40-mile-long (64 km) Russian military convoy heads for the capital city of Kyiv.

March 2: By a vote of 141 to 5, the United Nations condemns Russia's invasion of Ukraine.

March 10: A Ukrainian special forces drone unit halts the advancing Russian convoy.

March 16: Russia bombs a Mariupol theater, killing or injuring hundreds of civilians.

2022	February	March	April

February 21: Putin recognizes independence of Luhansk and Donetsk regions in eastern Ukraine.

February 24: Russia invades Ukraine.

April 1: The bodies of executed civilians are discovered in Bucha.

April 8: Russia bombs a crowded train station in Kramatorsk as thousands await transport to safer areas.

April 13: Ukrainian missiles sink the *Moskva*, the flagship of the Russian Black Sea Fleet.

April 19: Escalating attacks in Donbas, Russia begins the second phase of the war.

July 3: Russia takes control of the Luhansk region of Donbas.

July 9: A Russian missile attack on two apartment buildings kills at least forty-eight civilians

July 15: Ukraine's president, Volodymyr Zelenskyy, calls for international condemnation of Russia as a terrorist state.

May 18: Finland and Sweden apply for membership in the North Atlantic Treaty Organization.

May 19: Mariupol falls to Russia.

May 20: The United States approves $40 billion in humanitarian and military aid to Ukraine.

May 23: Following Ukraine's first war crimes trial, a Russian soldier is sentenced to life in prison.

May   **June**   **July**

June 16: By this date, more than 5 million Ukrainians have fled to other parts of Europe and another 8 million are internally displaced.

June 23: Russia occupies the eastern city of Sievierodonetsk.

June 25: The US High Mobility Artillery Rocket System is deployed, giving Ukraine long-range strike capability.

An Unprovoked Attack

The young Ukrainian couple originally planned to marry in May 2022. But on February 24, Yaryna Arieva and Sviatoslav Fursin said their wedding vows to the sound of air raid sirens. Arieva and Fursin had agreed that if the Russians attacked their country, they would marry as soon as possible. They tied the knot the day Russia began its fierce assault on Ukraine. The next day, Arieva and Fursin joined Ukraine's Territorial Defense Forces (TDF), volunteer citizen soldiers who are helping defend their country.

Russia's invasion was not unexpected. For months, President Vladimir Putin had been amassing his military might along the Russia-Ukraine border. By February, some 190,000 troops stood ready to invade at their leader's command. For Putin, giving that command would be the first step in his long-sought goal of bringing Ukraine back under Russian influence.

Justifying the Invasion

Russia and Ukraine share a long-running, often tempestuous relationship. For hundreds of years, they have fought over territory that is home to both Ukrainians and Russians. By 1922 they were united under the Communist banner of the Soviet Union, a forced alliance of Russia and other eastern European countries. The Soviet Union collapsed in 1991, freeing Ukraine to declare its independence that same year. Since that time, Ukraine has strengthened ties with the Western world, expressing interest in joining the North Atlantic Treaty Organization (NATO), a coalition of the United States and European nations dedicated to keeping peace in Europe. Russia, which shares a 1,282-mile (2,063 km) border with Ukraine, is not a NATO member, and Putin has long viewed Ukraine's quest to join NATO a threat to Russia.

Putin has voiced many other perceived threats to explain his invasion of Ukraine. He has claimed that Ukrainian saboteurs destroyed military vehicles on Russian soil. He has warned that Ukraine was preparing to use chemical weapons against Russian forces. He has accused Ukraine's leaders, who are based in the capital of Kyiv, of conducting systematic genocide against Russians living in their country—much like the Nazis once carried out against Europe's Jews. These are serious accusations—and, according to experts on Russia-Ukraine relations, not one of them is true. Putin has manufactured these and other falsehoods as an excuse to move against Ukraine. In a televised address on February 24, Putin announced the invasion, which he characterized as

On March 10, 2022, a Ukrainian drone captured this image of a Ukrainian ambush on a column of Russian tanks passing through a town near Ukraine's capital, Kyiv.

a special military operation. "The purpose of this operation is to protect people who . . . have been facing humiliation and genocide perpetrated by the Kiev [Kyiv] regime. To this end, we will seek to demilitarize and denazify Ukraine."[1]

Fierce Opposition

Russia is the largest nation in Eastern Europe, with a population of 145 million and military troops numbering 850,000. Russia's superior weapons and nuclear capability make it one of the world's most formidable military powers. In contrast, Ukraine's population is about 43 million; its military has about 200,000 active-duty personnel.

"We are going to fight for our land. We have to protect the people we love and the land we live on. I hope for the best, but I do what I can to protect my land."[2]

—Territorial Defense Forces volunteer Yaryna Arieva

Russia's invasion has caused immense suffering throughout Ukraine. Russian tanks and troops have assaulted Ukrainian cities, causing thousands of civilian casualties, including people tortured and murdered. Cruise missiles and cluster bombs have hit apartment buildings, schools, hospitals, and shopping centers, adding to the civilian death toll. Millions of Ukrainians have fled to neighboring countries in hopes of avoiding the advancing Russian forces. Though at first it seemed to the world that Putin would enjoy a swift and decisive victory, that has not happened. Ukraine has mounted a formidable defense thanks to its courageous people and their young and fearless president.

Volodymyr Zelenskyy, elected president of Ukraine in 2019 at the age of forty-one, rejected pleas to leave the country for his own safety. Instead, he has become a symbol of Ukrainian resistance. Zelenskyy's nightly speeches, which are posted on social media, have rallied the Ukrainian people and exposed the lies spread by Putin's constant disinformation efforts. He has called on his citizens to oppose the invasion and has entreated other nations to supply Ukraine with military equipment and monetary aid.

Ukrainian resistance immediately began fending off Russia's advances. In the early weeks of the war, Ukrainian special forces troops halted a 40-mile-long (64 km) column of Russian military vehicles headed for a planned assault on Kyiv. Six weeks into the war, the guided-missile cruiser *Moskva*, the flagship of Russia's Black Sea Fleet, was sunk by Ukrainian anti-ship cruise missiles. By April, Ukrainian forces had destroyed or captured more than four hundred Russian tanks as well as hundreds of other armored vehicles and artillery.

What Putin Wants

In the early months of the war, US military experts believed Putin's immediate military goal was the destruction of Ukraine's capital and the installation of a pro-Russian government. But other experts say Putin has a larger objective. Evelyn Farkas, a former US national security adviser, describes Putin's invasion of Ukraine as only the first step to regain control of the vast area of eastern Europe once dominated by Russia.

Ukrainians have heard Putin's self-aggrandizing statements and his repeated falsehoods. On a daily basis—for months—they have suffered his brutal attacks. Yet they remain fiercely loyal to their president and their country. They have shown remarkable courage in opposing the Russian invasion. "We are going to fight for our land," declared newlywed Yaryna Arieva as she and her husband registered for TDF duty. "We have to protect the people we love and the land we live on. I hope for the best, but I do what I can to protect my land."[2] Multiplied by thousands of like-minded Ukrainian citizens, such determination has made Putin's goal more difficult and its outcome less certain.

CHAPTER ONE

Russia and Ukraine: A Troubled History

With their dragon-headed longships and formidable combat skills, the Vikings of Scandinavia were for centuries the scourge of Europe. In the ninth century, a Viking named Rurik arrived in the eastern European city of Novgorod. Rurik was a prince of a Scandinavian people called the Rus. His descendants established a political state centered in the city of Kyiv. This state, known as Kyivan Rus, encompassed an area of some 510,000 square miles (1,330,000 sq km) in eastern Europe. It was a federation of several ethnic groups, mainly eastern Slavic peoples, and its vast area included what today are Russia and Belarus. Ukraine, a state whose name means "Borderland," was located on the frontier of Kyivan Rus. Today, these three nations consider Kyivan Rus the land of their common origin.

Kyivan Rus became prosperous because of its location on major European and Asian trade routes. But political upheaval and changing alliances ultimately caused a gradual decline of its power, especially in Ukraine. Western Ukraine was ruled by various invading nations, including Austria and Poland, while its eastern regions fell under Russian domination. By the eighteenth century, most of Ukraine had become part of the vast Russian Empire, which stretched from the Baltic Sea to the Pacific Ocean.

The Russian Empire ended in 1917 with the abdication of the last of the Russian czars and was replaced by a Communist government. In 1922, Ukraine was one of four independent Socialist republics that formed the Communist Union of Soviet Socialist Republics (USSR), also known as the Soviet Union. After Russia, Ukraine was the second-largest nation in the Soviet sphere.

The totalitarian leaders of the Soviet Union sought to spread the Communist ideology across eastern Europe and in other parts of the world. After World War II, it would confront the United States and its democratic allies in a decades-long political and military stalemate.

East Versus West

The years after the war witnessed two great world powers—the United States and the Soviet Union—heading alliances of nations in a global political struggle known as the Cold War. Led by the United States, the Western European powers were committed to limiting the Soviet Union's spread of communism in Eastern Europe.

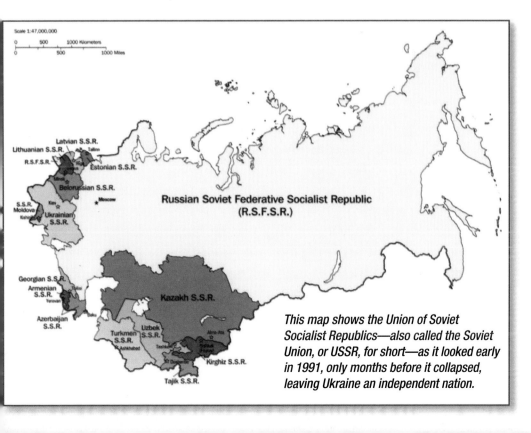

This map shows the Union of Soviet Socialist Republics—also called the Soviet Union, or USSR, for short—as it looked early in 1991, only months before it collapsed, leaving Ukraine an independent nation.

To defend their nations against aggression, each side established an organization for mutual defense. The West created NATO in 1949, and at the beginning of 2022 it encompassed thirty Western nations. NATO's treaty declares that an attack on any member nation would be considered an attack on all NATO members. The Soviet Union's answer to NATO was the Warsaw Treaty Organization, usually called the Warsaw Pact, which was created in 1955. The Warsaw Pact comprised seven Soviet-controlled nations, including Ukraine, in an alliance designed to provide a counterbalance to NATO.

Although the two sides never directly engaged in armed conflict (hence the name *Cold War*), several incidents brought the United States and the Soviet Union close to igniting dangerous confrontations. In 1962, for example, Soviet nuclear missiles were installed in Cuba, just 90 miles (145 km) from Florida. This was a response to the United States placing missiles in NATO member Turkey that could hit Moscow. Fears of World War III ultimately subsided when both sides agreed to remove their missiles.

The Cold War lasted more than four uneasy decades, but by the 1990s, the Soviet Union was in decline. Failed government reforms, a weak economy, and unrestrained military spending caused the Soviet Union to collapse in 1991. As a result, Ukraine and the other former Soviet nations became independent republics. The Warsaw Pact was disbanded that same year, and many member nations of the alliance joined NATO. Another consequence of the Soviet Union's collapse was that some 30 million Russians were living in nations no longer controlled by Russia. This led to friction between Ukraine's Russian and Ukrainian populations.

Ukraine is a nation divided by language. About two-thirds of its people (primarily in the West) speak Ukrainian, and one-third (mostly in the East and South) speak Russian. Partisan loyalty closely follows the language: eastern Ukrainians are supportive of Russia and its political aims, but western Ukrainians consider themselves European and are more suspicious of Russia and its motivations. This "split personality" has kept Ukraine from becoming a strong, unified nation able to establish its own destiny.

Complications of the Soviet Breakup

In the years after the Soviet collapse, Russia struggled to improve its deteriorating economy and contend with social upheavals. Boris Yeltsin, who was elected to Russia's new office of president in 1991, brought democracy to Russia and tried to improve the nation's economy. But Yeltsin's failed fiscal reforms, a hostile legislature, and two wars against rebels in the former Soviet nation of Chechnya took a toll both on his popularity and his health. On December 31, 1999, Yeltsin resigned. He chose Vladimir Putin to be his successor and acting president. Putin, a former Russian intelligence officer, had earlier been appointed by Yeltsin to the office of prime minister, a position of power second only to the Russian president. Now Yeltsin was bestowing on Putin the nation's most powerful position. Three months later, on March 26, 2000, Putin was elected to his first term as president of Russia.

In his early years as president, Putin helped strengthen Russia's economy and improve relations with the United States and the nations of western Europe. Yet he often expressed a longing for Russia's return to its former glory and lamented its demise. In a 2005

This photo, taken in 1999, shows outgoing Russian president Boris Yeltsin (on right in fur hat) shaking hands with Vladimir Putin, then Russia's prime minister and soon to be president. Over time, Putin accumulated more and more power.

speech, Putin declared, "The collapse of the Soviet Union was a major geopolitical disaster of the century. As for the Russian nation, it became a genuine drama. Tens of millions of our co-citizens and compatriots found themselves outside Russian territory. Moreover, the epidemic of disintegration infected Russia itself."[3]

Although Ukraine had gained its independence after the breakup of the Soviet Union, its pro-Russia president, Viktor Yanukovych, began to establish closer ties with Russia. Many Ukrainians objected. In February 2014, demonstrators against Yanukovych's policies began protesting in Kyiv. Yanukovych was ultimately removed from office and replaced by a more moderate interim president. Putin considered Ukraine's new government illegitimate and ordered Russian troops to invade Crimea, a peninsula in southern Ukraine. A poll taken in March showed that about 70 percent of people living in Crimea supported joining Russia.

Ukraine Becomes a Battleground

After Russia officially annexed Crimea in March 2014, the Western world condemned that action as illegal. Then, in April, pro-Russian separatists seized several state buildings in the Donetsk and Luhansk oblasts (administrative divisions similar to US states) in an industrial region of eastern Ukraine known as Donbas. Pro-

The Importance of Crimea

Extending into the Black Sea from southern Ukraine, the Crimean Peninsula was once the home of the Crimean Tatars, an Asian ethnic people who were indigenous to the region. Soviet leader Joseph Stalin deported the Tatars from Crimea in 1944, and it became mostly populated by Russians. Since that time, Russia has considered Crimea as part of its territory.

Crimea holds an important strategic place in the Russian sphere. Its major Black Sea port is Sevastopol, a warmwater port that can operate year-round, unlike northern ports that freeze in the winter. Sevastopol is home to the Russian Black Sea Fleet, which projects Russian naval power around the region. It is also a gateway to the trade routes of the Mediterranean Sea and the Atlantic Ocean beyond. Perhaps most important for Putin, control of Crimea is a way to keep the balance of power in the region stable between NATO and Russia.

When Russia officially annexed Crimea in 2014, it sent a signal to the West that the Ukrainian territory is part of Russia. The invasion of 2022 confirmed that Putin will fight to defend his claim.

testing the new Ukrainian government, the separatists were soon joined by Russian soldiers and tanks. Considering these protests as acts of terror, Ukraine responded by sending an anti-terrorist military force to stem the incursion. Two peace agreements were negotiated to stop the fighting, but neither fully ended hostilities. By 2022, the conflict had continued for more than eight years, resulting in more than fourteen thousand deaths.

Ukraine had become a battleground, pitting Ukrainians longing for independence against a Russian leader poised to revive his country's former power over the nations of eastern Europe. "Ukraine has always been a sore spot for Vladimir Putin," says William Pomeranz, an expert in Russia's politics and economy. "He does not recognize its independence and its right to be a country."[4] In 2008, Putin expressed his view of Russia's relationship with Ukraine when he told President George W. Bush, "You understand, George, that Ukraine is not even a state! What is Ukraine? A part of its territory is Eastern Europe, and part, and a significant part, is donated by us!"[5]

Putin did not hide his contempt for an independent Ukraine. But a new era in Ukraine began in 2019 when a man committed to Ukrainian independence was elected president. As a former actor and comedian, the new president was inexperienced in politics. What Volodymyr Zelenskyy lacked in experience, however, he displayed in courage and a vision for the future of Ukraine.

> "Ukraine has always been a sore spot for Vladimir Putin. He does not recognize its independence and its right to be a country."[4]
>
> —Kennan Institute director William Pomeranz

> "Ukraine is not even a state! What is Ukraine? A part of its territory is Eastern Europe, and part, and a significant part, is donated by us!"[5]
>
> —Russian president Vladimir Putin

A Novice President

Zelenskyy was born in 1978 to Jewish parents living in the city of Kryvyi Rih, located in southeastern Ukraine. Zelenskyy eventually developed an interest in performing, and in 2003 he established his own television production company. One of his productions, a popular series called *Servant of the People*, sparked his interest in politics. In the show, Zelenskyy starred as a high school teacher whose angry rant against government corruption went viral, ultimately thrusting him into the nation's presidency. In a case of life imitating art, Zelenskyy ran for president of Ukraine in 2019, naming his political party "Servant of the People." He was elected president in a landslide victory, earning an astonishing 73 percent of the vote.

Improving relations between Ukraine and Russia was Zelenskyy's first priority as president. As fighting in Donbas dragged on, Zelenskyy was reluctant to send more Ukrainian troops there and risk a larger conflict with Russia. "How many of them will die?" asked Zelenskyy during a 2019 *Time* magazine interview. "Hundreds of thousands, and then an all-out war will start, an all-out war in Ukraine, and then across Eastern Europe."[6] Zelenskyy met

Having been elected as Ukraine's president in a landslide victory in which he received 73 percent of the vote, on May 20, 2019, Volodymyr Zelenskyy addresses the Ukrainian parliament in his inauguration speech.

The Revolution of Dignity

Kyiv's Independence Square (Maidan Nezalezhnosti) has been the site of political demonstrations on and off since Ukraine became independent in 1991. In November 2013, when Ukraine's pro-Russian president, Viktor Yanukovych, abruptly canceled his country's plan to join the European Union, protests erupted at Maidan. Those protests continued for months. Then, in February 2014, the peaceful protests were shattered by government snipers firing into the crowd. More than one hundred people were killed. The protest, which came to be called the Revolution of Dignity, ended on February 21 of that year, when Yanukovych was removed from office and exiled to Russia.

Maidan is remembered as a symbol of Ukrainians fighting for their rights. But with his invasion in February 2022, Putin made it a symbol of his resolve to repress Ukraine. Rumors are circulating that he is planning to reinstate Yanukovych as Ukraine's president. "Putin is mocking the anniversary of the Revolution of Dignity," notes activist Svitlana Zalishchuk. "[He says] the choice you made in 2014, you think that you are already on the right path, but you didn't pay the price. And let's see where it goes, the path you chose."

Quoted in Haley Ott, "Eight Years After Pro-Democracy Protesters Were Killed in Kyiv, Ukraine Faces Greater Russian Threat," CBS News, February 20, 2022. www.cbsnews.com.

with Putin in December 2019, but little was accomplished to ease tensions between the two nations. "There are a lot of questions we haven't succeed[ed] to solve today,"[7] Zelenskyy commented. Putin was adamant that Russia remain in control of Donetsk and Luhansk as a buffer zone between Russia and Ukraine. In addition, Putin repeated his most important and unwavering demand: that Ukraine never join NATO.

Preparing for Invasion

By April 2021, the COVID-19 pandemic had killed almost 3 million people worldwide, US troops were preparing to leave Afghanistan, and some 435 miles (700 km) above Earth, a high-resolution satellite was taking photographs of disturbing military activity near Ukraine. Thousands of Russian troops and armored vehicles were seen amassing along the border of Russia and Ukraine. Dismissed by Russian military officials as merely a routine training exercise, the international community feared that the deployment—the largest since 2014—signaled preparation for an invasion of Ukraine. Although some Russian troops were eventually withdrawn, a further buildup in November brought Russia's military strength at the border to an estimated 100,000 troops. By February 2022, the Russian deployment had grown to approximately 190,000 troops, along with such tactical equipment as surface-to-air missile launchers, tanks and armored vehicles, and a fleet of warships in the Black Sea.

Putin was preparing to carry out a plan to make Russia once more into the great power it had been in the era of the czars. He envisioned himself as a new Peter the Great, the Russian emperor whose eighteenth-century wars expanded Russia's territory and influence. Putin is "reliving the Russian imperial dream," says Kyle Wilson, a researcher at the Centre for European Studies at the Australian National University. "And the man who made Russia into an imperial empire was Peter the Great."[8] Putin's goals for the war were to halt NATO's spread into eastern Europe, beginning with Ukraine, and to send a message to other former Soviet states that there would be consequences if they allied themselves with the West.

To justify the massive buildup of armed forces at Ukraine's eastern border, Putin declared that the pro-Russian population in Donbas was in danger of extermination by Ukrainian forces. "You and I know what is happening in Donbas," he remarked in a presidential council meeting. "It certainly looks like genocide."[9] Ukrainian officials denounced the charge as absolutely false, calling it a pretext for escalating Russian aggression.

On February 21, 2022, Putin announced that Russia now recognized the separatist-held provinces of Donetsk and Luhansk as independent states. Blaming Ukrainian retaliation against the pro-Russian rebels in these oblasts, Putin claimed that "the aggressive and nationalistic regime that seized power in Kyiv . . . and those who then embarked on the path of violence, bloodshed and lawlessness . . . do not recognize now any solution to the Donbas issue other than a military one."[10]

Three days later, Putin launched his own military solution.

CHAPTER TWO

Russia Invades Ukraine

In the predawn hours of February 24, 2022, residents of several Ukrainian cities were jolted awake by the sounds of explosions rumbling through the darkness. The invasion that many believed Putin would not dare attempt had begun, initiating the largest military action in Europe since World War II. Bombs, missiles, and attack helicopter fire brought destruction throughout Ukraine in preparation for a ground invasion. Although the initial attacks targeted military installations, many nonmilitary structures came under fire—destroying civilian infrastructure and causing large numbers of civilian casualties.

Russian troops and tanks began the ground invasion on three fronts. In the North, forces advanced into Ukraine across the borders from Russia and Belarus, heading toward their goal of capturing Kyiv. In the East, the invasion centered on attacking Kharkiv, Ukraine's second-largest city, and the eastern industrial area of Donbas. Across the southern border, Russian forces from Crimea pushed into the interior of Ukraine, while amphibious raids from Russian vessels on the Black Sea targeted the port city of Odesa.

In the northern offensive, Russian soldiers mounted an assault on the inactive Chernobyl nuclear power plant, the site of a disastrous 1986 explosion and subsequent release of radioactive material. With a main road running from Chernobyl to Kyiv, securing the plant's site would provide a clear path to attack Kyiv. As tanks and troops surrounded the closed but still

dangerous facility, European officials expressed fears that the plant could again release harmful radioactive dust if struck by artillery or mortar fire. Although a radiation leak did not occur, Russian troops captured the power plant by the end of the first day.

That same day, 137 Ukrainian soldiers and civilians were killed and more than 300 were injured. Thousands of citizens in Kyiv and other cities sought shelter in basements and subway stations, taking with them a few personal belongings, such as sleeping bags, food, and even pets. Others fled to smaller, safer towns in the countryside. Many were not sure what they would find at home once the shelling stopped. "I plan to return to my home when the alarm sirens finish," said lawyer Oleksandra Matviychuk from a shelter outside Kyiv. "If it's [still] a home. Last night the Russians shelled a housing block. These days will be difficult for us."[11]

Putin's Rationale

Shortly before the invasion began, Putin spoke to the people of Russia in a live television broadcast. Seated at a large desk with

Russian flags framing the background, Putin set forth his justification for the invasion:

> The people's republics of Donbas have asked Russia for help. . . . I made a decision to carry out a special military operation. The purpose of this operation is to protect people who, for eight years now, have been facing humiliation and genocide perpetrated by the Kyiv regime. To this end, we will seek to demilitarize and denazify Ukraine, as well as bring to trial those who perpetrated numerous bloody crimes against civilians, including against citizens of the Russian Federation.[12]

Putin's claims of "genocide" and the need to "denazify" Ukraine had no basis in fact. Experts worldwide have stated unequivocally that this statement (and others made by Putin to justify the invasion) represent a classic case of disinformation. Further, his description of the invasion as a "special military operation" instead of a war was an attempt to downplay its seriousness for the Russian people. Russian teachers and media outlets were warned not to use the words *war* or *invasion* to describe the hostilities. As the Russian population was being fed their government's story of the invasion, the falling bombs and missile strikes told Ukrainians that they were indeed engaged in a war for their very existence.

"I made a decision to carry out a special military operation. The purpose of this operation is to protect people who, for eight years now, have been facing humiliation and genocide perpetrated by the Kyiv regime."[12]

—Russian president Vladimir Putin

Zelenskyy Responds

As Russian forces advanced into Ukraine, speculation in Russia, Ukraine, and around the world turned to the whereabouts of President Zelenskyy. Russian propaganda reported that Zelenskyy, fearing for his life, had escaped the besieged capital. But Zelenskyy did not flee; instead, he turned to social media to reassure

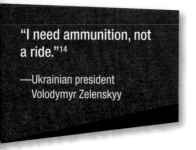
the Ukrainian people. Standing with his aides in front of Kyiv's presidential office building, Zelenskyy recorded a video on the Telegram messaging app on the second day of the invasion. "We are here," he said. "We are in Kyiv. . . . Our army is here, our civil society is here, we are all here. We are defending our independence, our state, and we will continue to do so."[13] Russian troops reportedly attempted to find Zelenskyy to kill him or take him hostage, but without success. When the United States offered to escort him to safety, he boldly asserted his resolve to stay and fight for his country, saying, "I need ammunition, not a ride."[14]

True to his word, Zelenskyy remained in Kyiv despite the danger to him and his family. "According to our information," he said, "the enemy has marked me as target number one, my family as target number two. They want to destroy Ukraine politically by destroying the head of state."[15] Typically wearing a dark green or brown T-shirt as a symbol of solidarity with his soldiers, Zelenskyy led his nation from underground bunkers. But he emerged frequently from safety to encourage his troops, and to show his support for the suffering Ukrainian people. In late May, Zelenskyy toured Kharkiv, where

The Will to Fight

One of the biggest surprises of the invasion of Ukraine was the ineffectiveness of the Russian forces on the battlefield. What was predicted to be a swift victory over Ukraine quickly turned into a stalemate in which the stronger Russian forces were often blocked by Ukrainian counterattacks. Observers cited low morale as part of Russia's problems.

When an army is fighting efficiently and its soldiers believe in its cause, morale will be high among the ranks and lead to better outcomes in battle. But according to the United Kingdom's Ministry of Defence, the conditions for high morale were lacking in the Russian forces in Ukraine. Equipment breakdowns, logistical problems causing food and ammunition shortages, and counterattacks by Ukrainian troops created low morale in the Russian ranks. Russian soldiers were seen looting Ukrainian grocery store shelves for food. Early failures to take Kyiv and other cities had Russian troops questioning their superiors' competence. Many abandoned their tanks and walked to the nearest Ukrainian town to surrender.

As the second phase of the war began in the East, Russia's fortunes improved; as casualties mounted, it was Ukraine's turn to suffer declining morale. If that trend continues, the outlook for Ukraine is grim.

Ukrainian forces had driven the Russians from the city. Amid the
rubble of more than two thousand buildings damaged by Russian
bombardment, Zelenskyy promised that the city would be rebuilt.

Targeting Kyiv

Kyiv was a major target for Russian forces. Seizing the capital
would effectively dismantle the government and bring a swift end
to the war. Urban war expert John Spencer explains that "[Russia] needed to get into the middle of Kyiv as quickly as possible
and raise the Russian flag over a government building. . . . At that
point you've won the war."[16] Some observers expected a Russian
victory within three or four days.

As part of the assault on Kyiv, Russian air and ground forces
engaged Ukrainian defenders in the Battle of Antonov Airport (also
called Hostomel), 10 miles (16 km) northwest of the city. Russia's
objective was to use the airport as the main staging area for assaults on Kyiv. Russian attack helicopters flying low from Belarus
provided escort for transport choppers bringing in hundreds of
paratroopers. The troops faced stiff resistance from the Ukrainian

military firing antiaircraft missiles, but after a two-day battle the Russians seized control of the airport. For weeks the two sides attacked and counterattacked, with the Ukrainian forces finally successful in driving back the invaders. By early April, the defeated Russians abandoned Antonov, leaving behind discarded military gear, weapons, and hulks of destroyed tanks. The airport had been damaged so badly that it was rendered unusable for further military operations.

The Siege of Mariupol

While Russian soldiers in Ukraine's northern region were fighting their way toward the capital, forces in the Southeast carried out an assault on the port city of Mariupol. Located in the Donetsk oblast, Mariupol lies on the coast of the Sea of Azov, which leads directly into the Black Sea and access to international maritime trade routes. Capturing Mariupol would create an unobstructed pathway for Russian troops in Crimea to join up with the pro-Russian separatist forces in Donbas. It would also prevent Ukrainian troops and civilians in the region from receiving food, arms, and other supplies via ocean routes.

From the beginning of the Russian invasion, Mariupol came under devastating artillery fire and aerial bombardment. Residents of the city took refuge wherever they could find shelter, including in a huge factory complex called the Azovstal Steel Plant. As Russian troops advanced to the city's outskirts, Ukrainian forces counterattacked, destroying Russian tanks and capturing enemy troops. But they could not stop the Russian onslaught, and hundreds of Ukrainian soldiers, some severely wounded, took shelter in the Azovstal plant. Ground artillery fire and aerial bombardment continued until, by late March, some 90 percent of Mariupol lay in ruins. Estimates of civilian deaths in the city ranged from five thousand to more than twenty thousand.

By May 20, Russian forces had gained nearly complete control of Mariupol, a much-needed success after the failure to take Kyiv. The Azovstal plant was the last refuge for Ukrainian soldiers and

Ukrainian citizens of all ages and walks of life seek shelter in a subway station in the capital city of Kyiv in late February 2022, only hours after the start of Russia's unprovoked invasion of their country. Fortunately for them, the Russian attempt to quickly seize Kyiv failed.

civilians trapped in the city. Instead of risking his dwindling supply of troops in an attempt to take over the factory, Putin established a blockade to deprive the defenders of food, water, and medical supplies. With no way to continue defending the Azovstal plant, Ukrainian military officials declared that the combat mission was over and the troops would be evacuated. "We hope that we will be able to save the lives of our guys," Zelenskyy said in a Telegram message. "I want to emphasize that Ukraine needs Ukrainian heroes alive."[17] The last Ukrainian troops in Azovstal, estimated at several hundred, were evacuated to Russian territory to receive care for the wounded and arrange a prisoner exchange with Russia. Civilians, many of whom had sheltered for two months in the factory, boarded buses to take them to a safer area.

The War in the East

Victory in the battle for Mariupol was a much-needed boost for Russian morale. But the failure to take Kyiv in February still loomed large for Russian military strategists. "Russia's assault into northern Ukraine ended in a costly failure,"[18] noted a report from the

High-Tech Weapons

The war in Ukraine has unleashed a new generation of weapons with a killing power far greater than its predecessors. Artillery and bombs of the twentieth century have given way to smart weapons, laser- and GPS-guided missiles, and drones that can autonomously seek and destroy unseen targets. These new weapons have pioneered new ways to kill.

One such weapon is the thermobaric missile, which can be launched from an armored vehicle or a handheld launcher. When the thermobaric missile hits its target, an initial small explosion releases a highly explosive mist of fuel that mixes with atmospheric oxygen. A second explosion then ignites this mixture, causing a massive lethal blast and shockwave. The explosive vapor can seep into buildings, tunnels, and shelters, causing massive damage and loss of civilian life.

Although manned aircraft have been used in combat since World War I, unmanned aerial vehicles (UAVs) are the wave of the future. The Bayraktar TB2 is a Turkish-made drone with impressive firepower. Operating at an altitude of 25,000 feet (7,600 m), it can fly for twenty-four hours straight and destroy enemy tanks with up to four laser-guided missiles. Ukraine has deployed fifty Bayraktar TB2s in the war against Russia.

United Kingdom's Ministry of Defence. Ukrainian counterattacks had repulsed Russian advances across the country and driven the enemy from much of the territory they had seized. Estimates of Russian casualties varied, ranging from about fifteen to thirty thousand dead in the first three months of the war.

Turning its attention to the East, Russia began its second phase of the war in April, stepping up its assault on the Luhansk and Donetsk oblasts in Donbas. Fierce bombardment and shelling devastated the area, destroying much of the infrastructure and causing thousands of casualties. "They have adopted this technique, which is a World War I technique fundamentally, of using artillery to just obliterate everything in front of them and then crawl over the rubble,"[19] said former professor of military history Frederick W. Kagan.

The city of Sievierodonetsk in Luhansk was a key target for Russian forces. Capturing the city would be an important step in the goal of controlling Luhansk and would give Russia another powerful symbolic victory. The assault on Sievierodonetsk was overwhelming. According

> "They have adopted this technique, which is a World War I technique fundamentally, of using artillery to just obliterate everything in front of them and then crawl over the rubble."[19]
>
> —Former professor of military history Frederick W. Kagan

to Serhiy Gaidai, the governor of Luhansk, "They shell for several hours—for three, four, five hours—in a row and then attack. Those who attack die. Then shelling and attack follow again, and so on until they break through somewhere."[20] Thousands of residents fled the city, which once had a population of more than one hundred thousand, now reduced to some twelve to thirteen thousand huddled in shelters and basements.

Russian troops finally gained ground in the Donbas in June and July. On June 24, Sievierodonetsk fell to Russia, representing its largest battlefield victory since Mariupol. The next Ukrainian city to fall was Lysychansk, the last obstacle to Russian control of Luhansk. On July 3, Russian troops occupied the city, setting the stage for taking over the entire Donbas region.

Russia's Relentless War

Despite these victories in the East, by mid-2022 the war dragged on, with an exhausted Russian army facing a Ukrainian military that showed remarkable courage. According to *USA Today*, by mid-July Russian forces had suffered some fifty thousand killed and wounded, as well as thousands of fighting vehicles and tanks destroyed. But Russia was not giving up. On July 16, Russia's defense minister ordered the Russian military to increase the intensity of its offensive, especially in the Donbas region.

Sources close to Moscow reported the possibility that Putin might order another assault on Kyiv, with the goal of winning the war by the fall of 2022. As of July, the outcome of the war was by no means assured. Ukraine's military and civilian forces were continuing their fight, led by their young but determined president. In 2018, while facing his first election, Zelenskyy had described his personal resolve. "I'm such a guy," he said, "that if I get involved in a battle, I usually don't get out of it. I can lose, but go out in the middle of it . . . no. The white flag is not our flag."[21] At the time, he had no idea of the extreme pressures he and his country would face. If Ukraine's early response to Russia's unprovoked war is any indication, in 2022, Russia is unlikely to see its adversary flying a white flag.

CHAPTER THREE

Ukraine Fights Back

On February 22, as war with Russia loomed on the horizon, President Zelenskyy announced the call-up of Ukrainian military reservists to prepare for a Russian invasion. Zelenskyy said he was still hoping for a diplomatic solution to the crisis, but Ukraine needed to prepare for the worst. His hopes for peace were crushed two days later when Russia launched its invasion. As bombs and missiles pounded Ukrainian cities and Russian troops pushed across the border, Zelenskyy announced a full mobilization of the Ukrainian military. Ukrainian men aged eighteen to sixty were subject to conscription, or being drafted into the armed forces. They were forbidden to leave the country to avoid the draft. In cities across Ukraine, men young and old, beginning with those who had military experience, lined up to register for military service. They did not know where they would be sent, and some were reluctant to go, but they knew that they were going to fight for their country. "Now is no time for feelings," said Viktor, a fifty-eight-year-old conscript. "If it is necessary to go to war, then that's what it is. We are proud to do this for our country."[22]

By the end of the first day of the invasion, Zelenskyy praised the courage of his army:

Men and women, our defenders! You are brilliantly defending the country from one of the most powerful countries in the world. Today Russia attacked the entire territory of our state. And today our defenders have done a lot. They defended almost the entire territory of Ukraine, which suffered direct blows. They regained territory that the enemy managed to occupy.[23]

When Russia began its invasion, Ukraine had an active military strength of about 200,000, along with 250,000 reservists. Russia's ground forces outnumbered Ukraine's, and it had more fighter jets, more tanks, and more attack helicopters. Despite the disparity in military might, Ukraine's tenacious soldiers were able to thwart the Russian advance on several fronts, claiming victory in battles for Kyiv, Kharkiv, and other Ukrainian cities. A particularly impressive success involved one of Russia's most advanced guided-missile cruisers on the Black Sea.

> "Now is no time for feelings. If it is necessary to go to war, then that's what it is. We are proud to do this for our country."[22]
>
> —Ukrainian conscript Viktor

Sinking the *Moskva*

The Black Sea lies between Europe and Asia, bordered by several countries, including Ukraine to the north and Russia to the east. This strategic body of water serves several purposes. For Russia, it provides a buffer zone against NATO nations and an economic trade route through the Mediterranean Sea to the Atlantic Ocean. For Ukraine, it is an equally important trade route. To lose its ports on the Black Sea would render Ukraine a landlocked nation deprived of ocean trade routes.

The flagship of Russia's Black Sea Fleet was the guided-missile cruiser *Moskva*, the largest and most powerful ship in the fleet and a symbol of pride for the Russian navy. On April 13, the *Moskva* was sailing south of the Ukrainian port of Odesa when it was struck by two R-360 Neptune anti-ship missiles. Launched by Ukrainian troops from shore, the missiles exploded on the port side of the *Moskva*, and fire soon engulfed the vessel. The next morning the ship sank, after its crew was reportedly evacuated.

The *Moskva* was the largest Russian warship to be sunk since World War II.

Ukraine celebrated its victory. In Russia, the government-controlled news media blamed the sinking on an accidental explosion of the ship's ammunition stores, followed by a storm at sea. There was no mention of the Ukrainian missile strike. Despite denial of the true cause of the disaster, Putin knew too well the cost of the sinking. Besides striking a blow to Russia's pride in the Black Sea Fleet, the loss caused a setback in its wartime capabilities. Losing the *Moskva* meant losing a major missile-launching platform that would have provided support for ground forces in combat operations. It also demonstrated that Ukrainian forces could successfully attack Russia's sea power from land-based locations. If the Russians once thought their Black Sea Fleet was invincible, they now knew that they had underestimated their adversary.

Despite numerous successes achieved by the Ukrainian armed forces, battlefield casualties mounted. By mid-May, the Ukrainian military had suffered up to eleven thousand combat

A postage stamp issued in late May 2022 in the western Ukrainian city of Lviv celebrates Ukraine's recent sinking of the Russian guided-missile cruiser Moskva *in the Black Sea. The caption on the stamp reads, "Russian warship—Done!"*

A Teenage Drone Warrior

As a convoy of Russian tanks and trucks headed toward Kyiv from the west, Ukrainian forces desperately needed to determine the enemy's exact location. Drones would be the perfect tool to collect this information, but early in the conflict the Ukrainian military had none. After putting out an appeal for civilian drone pilots, many answered the call—including fifteen-year-old Andrii Pokrasa. The youngest of the volunteers, Pokrasa had extensive experience using drones for aerial photography. His skills were just what the military needed.

One night, Pokrasa began flying his drone in search of the convoy. When one of the vehicles momentarily turned on its headlights, the drone captured its image and GPS coordinates. Pokrasa relayed the information to Ukrainian forces, which destroyed the column with artillery fire. "I was very scared," Pokrasa said, "but if I didn't help them, the Russians could be here in a day."

Although hailed as a hero, Pokrasa now must deal with the harsh reality of war. "I was so happy that I helped, but also there were people in those Russian vehicles. They were occupiers, but still people. I don't know how to explain how I feel about it."

Quoted in Global News, "How a 15-Year-Old Ukrainian Drone Pilot Helped Destroy a Russian Army Column," YouTube video, June 6, 2022. www.youtube.com/watch?v=AOHkJbjmZRU.

dead and eighteen thousand wounded—about 10 percent of their total forces. (Russia was reported to have suffered more than thirty-five thousand casualties.) In a television interview on May 31, Zelenskyy said, "We are losing 60 to 100 soldiers per day killed in action and something around 500 people as wounded in action."[24] Ukraine needed to employ all means of resistance to fight its larger and stronger enemy, and Zelenskyy called on Ukrainian civilians to do their part.

Civilian Warriors

The Territorial Defense Forces (TDF) is a component of the Ukrainian military similar to the National Guard in the United States. Ukrainian citizens who volunteer receive training while continuing their normal employment. In a national emergency such as the Russian invasion, they can be called up for duty under the leadership of professional soldiers. Volunteers come from all age groups and all walks of life, from farmers and merchants to computer programmers and truck drivers. By early March, some one hundred thousand volunteers had joined the ranks of the TDF.

In mid-February 2022, Ukrainian civilians use wooden replicas of rifles to train for actual combat. President Zelenskyy repeatedly praised the thousands of ordinary citizens who answered the government's call to step forward and help defend the nation.

By performing routine tasks such as patrolling city streets, staffing checkpoints, and delivering food and water to civilians sheltering in basements, TDF volunteers free up regular combat soldiers to battle the enemy. But their training also includes weapons instruction to prepare them to defend their towns and cities if necessary. And from the beginning of the invasion, they have proved their worth in combat: TDF units played an important part in the battles for Kyiv and Kharkiv.

The Peoples' Resistance

While the TDF created a second line of defense behind Ukraine's regular army, thousands of other civilians were also stepping up to defend their country. On a snowy February afternoon, a group of young volunteers gathered at a former factory in the western Ukrainian city of Lviv and created a makeshift assembly line within the building's brick walls. The volunteers were soon busy assembling a new product in the old structure's basement: anti-tank bombs, otherwise known as Molotov cocktails. Simple in design, these explosive devices can be made by unskilled civilians. And they are effective in war. When a Molotov cocktail is thrown toward a tank or other armored vehicle, the resulting explosion and fire penetrates the vehicle's air intake ports and destroys the target's engine.

Such civilian resistance has played an important role in the history of warfare. World War II resistance groups in France, Belgium, the Netherlands, and other occupied nations formed underground movements to hinder the Nazi occupiers. After the Russian invasion of 2022, Ukrainian citizens similarly stepped up to support their army. "While Ukraine's armed forces are proving themselves capable," says US Army major Walter Haynes, "no resistance can succeed without an effective auxiliary [of citizens in occupied areas] and underground. The civil element will be essential in the current conflict."[25]

The civilian Molotov cocktail makers were responding to the Ministry of Defense of Ukraine's plea for citizens to "prepare firebombs and bring down the occupiers."[26] Instructions on how to make the devices were broadcast on television. The volunteers, who ranged in

A Railroad War

Railroads have played an important role in warfare since the nineteenth century, transporting troops, weapons, food, and supplies to the battlefields. In the Russian invasion of Ukraine, rail lines between Belarus and Ukraine became a pathway for the invading forces. But Belarusian activists who oppose Russia's influence in their own country have been secretly working to sabotage the rail lines. Their goal is to delay, and ultimately stop, the invading Russian army.

During World War II, Belarusian saboteurs destroyed Nazi railroad infrastructure. When Putin deployed Russian troops in Belarus in advance of the invasion, anti-Russian partisans went into action. The world has changed since World War II, and so has technology. Modern-day rail warriors are focused on technical targets. A hacker group called the Cyber Partisans attacked railroad signal control boxes and computer systems, cutting off rail traffic between Belarus and Ukraine. "It was a way to show that Belarusians don't approve of the Russian army's presence on our territory," says Cyber Partisans spokesperson Yuliana Shemetovets. "We're trying to do as little damage as possible to infrastructure that affects regular people."

Quoted in Meduza, "The Guerrilla War on Belarus's Railways," July 5, 2022. https://meduza.io/en.

age from eighteen to thirty-five, labored with the knowledge that they were helping the war effort. "The youth are moved by this patriotic spirit," explains twenty-five-year-old Rodion Kadatskyi. "Everyone now realizes what he or she is capable of doing."[27]

Nonlethal Resistance

While Molotov cocktails were being made and transported to the front lines, more civilians were implementing other, less lethal but equally important methods to slow the Russian assault. To confuse the invaders, people throughout Ukraine removed street signs and plaques bearing town and village names. Citizens skilled in metal-work created anti-tank barriers known as "hedgehogs" by welding I beams or railroad tracks together in an X-shaped configuration. Placed on roads leading to major urban areas, the hedgehogs slow down or stop enemy tanks and armored vehicles, making them vulnerable to artillery fire or Molotov cocktail attacks.

The residents of a town in western Ukraine employ an assembly-line-like approach to manufacturing Molotov cocktails. These homemade bombs can be extremely effective against several different kinds of armored vehicles.

In many cities, groups of citizens put themselves in harm's way by gathering on roads and at city entrances to block Russian advances. Volunteers also filled thousands of sandbags and transported them by truck to block roads and protect valuable monuments and other cultural sites. Workers operating cranes placed heavy cement blocks on roadways to further delay the Russians' progress. Along with these physical strategies, some highly trained volunteers used their computing skills in a real-life game of high-tech war.

Cyberwarfare

Dave is a software engineer in Ukraine working for a US-based information technology (IT) consulting company. Since his normal job routine has been interrupted by the Russian invasion, he spends hours every day being a cyberwarrior. He is one of more than three hundred thousand volunteer tech workers—both inside and outside of Ukraine—who have joined a group on Telegram known as the IT Army of Ukraine. Its mission: to disrupt the websites of Russian banks, government agencies, businesses, and media companies using a strategy known as distributed denial of service, or DDoS. Target sites to be hacked are shared on Telegram; cyberwarriors then mount a massive simultaneous cyberattack, inundating the sites with traffic to knock them offline.

Hackers have also used their skills to counter Russian propaganda. Russian citizens are only told what Putin wants them to hear through government-controlled media. May 9 is Victory Day in Russia, a day that celebrates Russia's World War II victory over Nazi Germany. But television coverage of the day's parade did not go quite as planned, as hackers replaced on-screen captions with a message to the Russian people: "On your hands is the blood of thousands of Ukrainians and their hundreds of murdered children. TV and the authorities are lying. No to war."[28] Although the hackers were not identified, the protest broke through the Russian propaganda barrier.

Attacking from Above

In an unsettling video from an aerial drone, a bomb is seen plummeting toward a Russian tank. A sudden flash and explosion, and the tank is engulfed in flames, depriving Russia of one more weapon of war. The tank was destroyed by an elite team of civilians working with the Ukrainian Ground Forces to deliver destruction in the form of drones carrying small but deadly bombs. Called Aerorozvidka (meaning "Air Reconnaissance"), the team is a nongovernmental organization. According to the organization's website, it "exemplifies the direct engagement of civil society in repelling aggression against Ukraine."[29]

Aerorozvidka was formed in 2014 after Russia annexed Crimea and hostilities in Donbas broke out. Eager to help in the fight, volunteers with backgrounds in engineering, IT, and drone operations modified off-the-shelf drones for aerial surveillance. Today, Aerorozvidka operates in concert with Ukraine's military, using crowdsourcing to finance its operations. It builds its own custom drones as well as weaponizes commercial drones for surveillance and aerial bombardment. A major weapon in its drone arsenal is the R-18, an octocopter designed and built by Aerorozvidka volunteers. This menacing-looking device is driven by eight propellers and can carry two 11-pound (5 kg) bombs to a target up to 2.5 miles (4 km) away. Drones such as the R-18 have shown themselves to be valuable weapons from the outset of the invasion.

Killing a Convoy

During the first week of the invasion, Russian artillery and missiles relentlessly pounded Kyiv, destroying both military and civilian targets. On February 28, Ukrainian military intelligence discovered a disturbing new threat. Reconnaissance satellite images revealed that a 40-mile-long (64 km) column of Russian military vehicles was heading for the capital city. Originating in Belarus, the convoy consisted of Russian tanks, military transport vehicles, and heavy artillery, along with some fifteen thousand battle-tested Russian troops. Had it reached Kyiv, the city would have quickly fallen.

But waiting in the surrounding forests were Aerorozvidka troops ready to strike. Using rugged all-terrain vehicles called quad bikes for speed and mobility, they launched a nighttime drone attack on the convoy. Aerorozvidka usually attacks at night, when enemy troops are sleeping and darkness hides the drones' approach. The unit commander, Lieutenant Colonel Yaroslav Honchar, recalls, "This one little unit in the night destroyed two or three vehicles at the head of this convoy, and after that it was stuck. They stayed there two more nights, and [destroyed] many vehicles."[30]

The convoy halted about 19 miles (31 km) from Kyiv, the destroyed vehicles blocking the road from further progress. Many units of the convoy broke away and set up new positions in the surrounding forests, but others remained stuck on the road. Unable to move forward, the mechanized column abandoned its mission. Without the reinforcements and mechanized weapons that the column would have provided, Russia's expected swift victory over Kyiv became a massive failure.

The fact that Ukrainians are risking their lives to challenge the Russian aggressors may be the key to a Ukrainian victory. Maciej Bartkowski, an author and expert on civil resistance, agrees. "Putin's belief that Ukrainians would rather go home and do nothing in the face of military aggression may be his biggest and politically most costly miscalculation."[31]

> "Putin's belief that Ukrainians would rather go home and do nothing in the face of military aggression may be his biggest and politically most costly miscalculation."[31]
>
> —Civil resistance expert Maciej Bartkowski

CHAPTER FOUR

Humanitarian Tragedies of the War

The railroad station in the southeastern Polish town of Przemysl is a beautiful, historic building. Completed in 1860, its gilded interior incorporates paintings, antique chandeliers, and murals of the town, giving it the appearance of a lavish royal palace. Located less than 10 miles (16 km) from the Ukrainian border, it is the first stop for hundreds of thousands of Ukrainians fleeing the horrors of the Russian invasion.

By early March, ten to twenty thousand Ukrainian refugees were arriving at the Przemysl station every day. The trip to safety could be a grueling one. "It was hell," says Ali, who was in Kyiv studying to become a dentist. "Imagine standing for two days. No access to normal things like hygienic products, food, [and] water half the time."[32] As an Iraqi, Ali was allowed to leave Ukraine. Male Ukrainian citizens, however, were required by law to remain in the country, awaiting a call-up to fight. Thus, the trains that departed from Lviv and other cities were mostly filled with women, infants, and children; none could be sure if they would ever go home again.

Displaced Ukrainians

The Russian invasion of Ukraine created one of the worst humanitarian crises in modern history. With Russian artillery and air strikes devastating cities across Ukraine, individuals and families who lost their homes hastily packed what few possessions they could and set out to escape to safer areas. According to figures compiled by the United Nations, by June 16 more than 5 million Ukrainians had fled to nations across Europe. Most of these refugees went to Poland, but others traveled to Romania, Hungary, Germany, the Czech Republic, and elsewhere. These nations are members of the European Union, which has declared that refugees from Ukraine will be allowed to stay and work for up to three years.

Not all displaced Ukrainians fled their homeland; about 8 million people left their homes in hopes of finding safety in other parts of Ukraine. These internally displaced people sought refuge in the relatively safe western part of Ukraine as the Russians switched their military operations eastward. Although still living in their own country, the internal refugees still suffered the effects of the war, as Pascal Hundt, head of the International Committee of the Red

A Ukrainian woman and her boyfriend say their heartfelt goodbyes in Lviv shortly before his deployment to fight in the war's front lines. The conflict has separated many thousands of loved ones, including members of entire families, often with no guarantee they will ever be reunited.

Cross in Ukraine, explains: "We see people arriving in different parts of Ukraine from cities like Mariupol, deeply traumatized by what they have been through. The relief of having escaped the horrors of fighting is marred by the question: what is next? Some hope to be able to go back, while others have nothing to go back to."[33]

Water and electricity, two of the most important elements of modern society, have become scarce in parts of war-torn Ukraine. Russian air strikes have targeted power plants and water pumping stations, depriving Ukrainians of basic needs for survival. Citizens have endured living without running water or sanitary facilities, making health concerns a priority, especially for children. Unsafe water supplies can harbor bacteria and other organisms that can be harmful or fatal to children and health-compromised adults. Russian attacks damaged or destroyed more than four hundred medical facilities, making adequate medical care difficult or impossible. Damaged supplies of antibiotics meant that surgery could not be performed, and patients with serious diseases such as cancer and diabetes were deprived of necessary medications.

Schools and other refuges for children did not escape damage or destruction by Russian missiles and artillery fire. Nearly two-thirds of the 7.5 million children living in Ukraine were uprooted from their homes and taken to safer locations in Ukraine or across the border, often leaving other family members behind. For many children, safe passage did not come soon enough: more than 200 Ukrainian children have been killed since the start of the invasion, and hundreds more have suffered wounds. Child refugees, especially those who were sent to other countries unaccompanied, risked being taken advantage of by human traffickers who would attempt to exploit them for forced sex or labor.

As millions of Ukrainians fled to safety, millions more could not—or would not—leave their towns or cities. Motivated by loyalty, patriotism, or simply the inability to escape, these Ukrainians vowed to stand their ground and fight. Neither they nor the world at large could have imagined the atrocities committed by the Russians on those who stayed behind.

The Massacre at Bucha

Four days after the invasion of Ukraine began, Russian forces fighting their way toward Kyiv had advanced to the town of Bucha, about 15 miles (24 km) northwest of the capital. Fierce street battles raged and artillery damaged numerous civilian buildings as Russian tanks rolled through the city. The Russians occupied Bucha by the end of February, and for a month they terrorized the city's civilian population. Russian soldiers invaded apartments or smashed car windows looking for valuables to steal, and they forced citizens into their basements under threats of harm or death if they tried to leave.

Helping Refugees

Sixteen-year-old Ukrainian Anna Melnyk walks through the railroad station in Lviv, surrounded by hundreds of people displaced by the war. She wears a green vest with the word INFORMATION emblazoned on it, joining other volunteers in helping the confused and anxious people in the station know that this young stranger can help them. "Every day we try to volunteer," says Melnyk, "and every day to help another people how we can, to make our country better. Because when you volunteer you help, and you also help yourself. It motivates you."

Ten thousand refugees come through the Lviv station every day bound for Poland and other safe countries. Melnyk and volunteers like her offer refugees information on how to find their trains and what papers are needed. They hand out food and beverages, help the disabled, and assist those who must stay overnight before boarding a train. There are also orphans who need support and comfort amid the chaos of war.

Volunteering gives Melnyk a purpose beyond the frivolities of a teenager's world. "I'm glad that I can help and that I'm still alive. And I have a new day and a new chance to make something better."

Anna Melnyk, "From Class to Helping Families Flee" (video), in Hannah Allam, "Coming of Age in a War, One Ukrainian Teen Finds Her 'Mission,'" *Washington Post*, May 3, 2022. www.washingtonpost.com.

Ultimately, counterattacks by Ukrainian forces inflicted serious casualties on the Russian troops; by March 30, the Russians had withdrawn from Bucha. When Ukrainian soldiers regained control of the city, what they found in the aftermath of the Russian occupation was shocking.

The bodies of civilians littered the streets, their hands tied behind them with strips of white cloth, a clear indication that they had been murdered execution style. "In Bucha people were mainly just shot," says Taras Vyazovchenko, a city council member. "There are practically no accidental hits among the victims."[34] The deaths were seemingly inflicted randomly, with the Russians sometimes killing important city officials and at other times shooting ordinary people for any reason, or perhaps no reason. According to re-

On April 8, 2022, Ukrainian soldiers and civilian workers remove the bodies of their slain fellow citizens from a Russian-dug mass grave in the Ukrainian village of Bucha. There, Russian troops brutally massacred large numbers of largely defenseless Ukrainian civilians.

covery workers, civilians were shot as they tried to find food and water, while riding bicycles, or just setting foot out of their front doors. As Ukrainian troops and police combed the city for survivors, more bodies were found in basements and apartments where people had sought shelter. In some buildings, the basements were used as makeshift torture chambers where Ukrainian men were gathered to be brutalized and executed.

On March 31, satellite images revealed a mass grave on the grounds of Bucha's Church of St. Andrew and Pyervozvannoho All Saints. The grave stretched some 40 feet (12 m) in length, and from early estimates it contained around 150 bodies of civilians killed by the Russians. Soldiers and city officials began exhuming the bodies and transporting them to facilities where DNA tests could be used to determine the victims' identities.

Zelenskyy spoke out on the atrocities of Bucha, accusing the Russians of committing war crimes on Ukrainian civilians. "The world has already seen many war crimes," Zelenskyy said. "But it is time to do everything possible to make the war crimes of the Russian military the last manifestation of such evil on earth."[35]

"The world has already seen many war crimes. But it is time to do everything possible to make the war crimes of the Russian military the last manifestation of such evil on earth."[35]

—Ukrainian president Volodymyr Zelenskyy

Putin denied the accusation, stating that the videos and photographs of bodies in Bucha were staged fakes designed to put Russia in an unfavorable light. By mid-June, more than four hundred civilian deaths had been recorded in Bucha. The search for more bodies continued as Bucha's innocent victims were laid to rest. Sergiy Kaplychnyi, the head of Ukrainian rescue services, solemnly noted, "We'll bury them like humans."[36]

Violating the Rules of War

Among those who were repulsed by the reports of mass killings in Bucha was US president Joe Biden. Biden had previously accused

Putin of committing atrocities in Ukraine. On April 4, after learning about the massacre at Bucha, the president stated,

> You may remember I got criticized for calling Putin a war criminal. Well, the truth of the matter—you saw what happened in Bucha—he is a war criminal. But we have to gather the information . . . and we have to get all the detail [to] have a war crimes trial. This guy is brutal. And what's happening in Bucha is outrageous, and everyone's seen it.[37]

As strange as it may sound, war has laws that the combatants are obligated to follow. Known as international humanitarian law (IHL), it is a set of rules designed to prevent excessive human suffering and limit the use of weapons that may cause unnecessarily devastating effects. Violations of the rules of IHL are considered war crimes, and those who commit them can be punished by international tribunals.

Among the rules of war are prohibitions against the targeting or mistreatment of civilians; the use of torture or the humiliation of prisoners; withholding medical aid from the sick or injured; and destroying civilian buildings, crops, sources of water, and other necessities of life. Bucha was just one example of Russians disregarding the rules of war. In June, Zelenskyy's official representative in Crimea, Tamila Tasheva, reported that about six hundred civilians (including journalists and activists), were being held hostage in the Russian-occupied Kherson region in southern Ukraine. The rooms in which they were being held were described as torture chambers.

Targeting Civilians

Although some Ukrainians were being held in inhumane conditions, others were able to seek refuge in what they thought would be safer areas. In Mariupol, one of the city's main cultural sites, the Donetsk Academic Regional Drama Theater, became a refuge for more than one thousand people, including women and children. A sturdy, four-story building with thick walls and large basement,

Pictured are the remains of the historic Donetsk Academic Regional Drama Theater, in the Ukrainian city of Mariupol, after the Russians destroyed it in early March 2022. The strike killed an estimated three hundred Ukrainian civilians who were using the structure as a shelter.

it seemed a safe haven for those who crowded the theater's corridors, offices, prop storage spaces, and dressing rooms.

At around 10:00 a.m. on March 16, a Russian air strike destroyed the theater, reducing its interior to rubble and trapping hundreds under the debris. Several hundred survivors, most of whom had been sheltering in the basement, had to step on the injured and dead to escape. One wall of the theater collapsed on a makeshift outdoor field kitchen that had served food to the refugees. Around one hundred people standing near the kitchen were killed when the wall fell. In the chaos after the attack, officials estimated that about three hundred people had been killed. But as recovery efforts progressed, the estimate rose to some six hundred, making it the deadliest single attack of the war.

The bombing of the Donetsk Academic Regional Drama Theater was another example of Russia's disregard for the rules of war. As a civilian building, the theater was off-limits to an attack; theater employees even painted the Russian word for "children" in large white letters on the ground outside the theater as a warning to enemy aircraft. Predictably, the Russians denied any responsibility for the deadly attack. Instead, they falsely accused the Ukrainians of staging the bombing as a "false flag" operation, which is intended to disguise the perpetrator of an attack to pin blame on another. Russia said that Ukraine had bombed the theater to place the blame on Russia and encourage NATO to intervene. The Organization for Security and Co-operation in Europe determined that "this incident constitutes most likely an egregious violation of IHL and those who ordered or executed it committed a war crime."[38]

No Escape from Attack

Some of the people who were sheltering in the theater had previously escaped the destruction of a maternity hospital for women that also housed a unit for sick children. On March 9, the hospital had been hit by a Russian air strike, which killed at least three people, including a child, and injured seventeen. Russian officials gave conflicting accounts of the bombing, at first saying that all medical personnel and patients had left and that the hospital was being used by a Ukrainian militia unit. Later, the bombing was de-

Images of War

Photojournalists play a unique and vital role in documenting the tragedies and heroics of the Ukraine war. They contribute to understanding the motives and emotions of combatants and victims alike. "There is a reason to go into this work," says photographer Ron Haviv. "I don't believe that photography on its own can stop war, but it can have a positive effect. That's enough that I feel like my work is contributing."

Images from embattled Ukraine tell stories of loss, grief, and often callous brutality. Photographs of the bodies of Ukrainian civilians—executed with their hands tied behind their backs—revealed to the world the war crimes committed by the Russian forces. In another image, a wounded pregnant woman is carried on a stretcher from a bombed-out maternity hospital in Mariupol. Although taken to safety, both the woman and her baby died. The heartrending image showed millions around the world the horror of war on the most innocent victims.

The danger of being a war photographer does not deter Haviv. "I am inspired and I believe in the power of photography. That's why I am able to keep going back and doing this work."

Quoted in Michael Hedges, "Ukraine Through the Eyes of Experience," *AARP Bulletin*, June 2022, pp. 38–41.

scribed by Russian officials and conspiracy theorists as another false flag operation, with actors playing the victims.

A day before the hospital strike, a Russian missile had hit a railroad station in the eastern Ukrainian city of Kramatorsk. The station had been filled with as many as four thousand civilians, mostly women and children waiting to board trains that would take them to safety. Fifty-nine people were killed, a toll that included at least seven children. About one hundred people suffered injuries. Zelenskyy vowed to bring the Russians to justice in a future war crimes tribunal. "Like the massacre in Bucha," he said, "like many other Russian war crimes, the missile strike on Kramatorsk must be one of the charges at the tribunal, which is bound to happen."[39]

Ukraine's human rights commission reported that by early June, some thirty-eight thousand residential buildings across the country had been destroyed by Russian attacks, leaving hundreds of thousands of people homeless. In addition, nearly 2,000 schools had been damaged, with 180 totally demolished. According to statistics from the United Nations, as of June 20 there were 10,260 civilian Ukrainian war casualties, including 4,569 killed and 5,691 injured. The brazen and criminal assaults on innocent Ukrainian civilians shocked the world.

The World Reacts

On February 22, the day after Putin had officially recognized the independence of Luhansk and Donetsk in eastern Ukraine, President Biden expressed his outrage at the Russian leader's brazen move. "Who in the Lord's name does Putin think gives him the right to declare new so-called countries on territory that belonged to his neighbors? This is a flagrant violation of international law, and it demands a firm response from the international community."[40] That response took many forms, including the enacting of sanctions, supplying military equipment to Ukraine, and providing humanitarian aid to the millions of Ukrainians displaced by the war. After Russia's invasion, the world stood behind Ukraine, sending Putin a powerful message that his aggression would have far-reaching consequences.

International Denunciation

On March 2, the United Nations General Assembly overwhelmingly voted to condemn the Russian invasion of Ukraine, characterizing Putin's offensive as not simply the occupation of Ukraine, but an act of genocide. The international body called for Russia's immediate and total withdrawal of its military forces from Ukraine, and it expressed concern about the reports of attacks on Ukrainian civilians, schools, hospitals, and commercial buildings. A total of 141 member nations (out of 193) voted in favor of the resolution, with 35 abstaining and 5—Belarus, Eritrea, North Korea, Russia, and Syria—voting against.

When photographs and videos of Russia's actions in Bucha and other Ukrainian cities surfaced, it became clear that the war was creating one of the worst humanitarian crises in decades. Russia was suspended from the United Nations Human Rights Council, a group of forty-seven member states within the United Nations tasked with protecting human rights around the world. The suspension of Russia from the council removed the belligerent nation from a position of leadership in the area of human rights and sent a message to other nations that human rights violations will not be tolerated.

The global response to the invasion also hit Russia's consumer economy hard. By June 15, nearly one thousand multinational corporations had stopped doing business in the country. Among those corporations are Apple, Disney, General Motors, Ikea, McDonalds, Netflix, Pepsi-Cola, Starbucks, and TikTok. McDonalds, which had some 850 restaurants in Russia, closed all of their stores, eventually selling them to a Russian entrepreneur who will reopen them under a new name. Big Macs are gone, to be replaced with a similar sandwich, but there will no longer be Coke to wash it down, as Coca-Cola has also left Russia.

Numerous airlines no longer fly to Russia or through Russian airspace, including American, British Airways, Delta, Lufthansa, Japan Airlines, Virgin Atlantic, and United. In addition, the United States and other nations have banned Russian aircraft, both commercial and privately owned, from flying to or over their countries. Such actions further isolate Russia from the rest of the world and have a detrimental impact on its economy. But the world's nations were not done yet. Another way to penalize Russia came through sanctions.

Sanctioning Russia

Sanctions, or penalties, are used to punish nations for either exhibiting aggressive behavior against other nations or committing offenses against international law. Sanctions are usually imposed in the areas of finance, politics, energy, trade, or travel. Such

On April 12, 2022, as he had done several times in recent months, US president Joe Biden denounced the Russian invasion of Ukraine. He accused President Putin of genocide, the systematic destruction of an entire group or race of people.

penalties may be enacted by a single country (unilateral) or by a group of countries (multilateral), and they can target individuals, segments of industry, or entire nations. Sanctions are used to reprimand a nation and avoid the more serious action of going to war. But in some cases, sanctions are interpreted by the target nation as a belligerent act, escalating international tensions. Mikael Wigell, research director of the Finnish Institute of International Affairs, says that Russia "right now considers . . . the imposition of sanctions against Russia [as] acts of war. Russia speaks about 'Western economic warfare.'"[41]

Many Western nations had imposed sanctions on Russia when it annexed Crimea in 2014. With the invasion of Ukraine, these nations intensified their political and economic sanctions. "Putin is the aggressor," Biden declared, "and now he and his country will bear the consequences."[42] The United States, the United Kingdom, the twenty-seven-member

> "Putin is the aggressor, and now he and his country will bear the consequences."[42]
>
> —US president Joe Biden

European Union, Japan, Australia, and other nations placed restrictions on Russian government agencies, companies, and influential Russian individuals. Since the invasion, more than ten thousand specific sanctions have been imposed by the international community, with the goal of crippling Russia's economy to such an extent that continuing the war would be impossible.

On February 24, Biden announced sanctions against the Russian banking system that held some $1 trillion in assets. Russia was also denied access to its assets held in US banks. In March, the United States, European Union, United Kingdom, and Canada blocked seven Russian banks from the Society for Worldwide Interbank Financial Telecommunication (SWIFT). SWIFT helps facilitate electronic financial transactions between nations; without it, Russia was cut off from the global banking community.

Along with major banks, sanctions were imposed on both industries and individuals. Semiconductors and other electronic components have been banned from export to Russia, as have drones and their associated parts and software. Airplanes, repair parts, and equipment are also sanctioned. The United States and Germany took steps to prevent the opening of a new underwater

Targeting Russian Oligarchs

A group of corrupt Russian businessmen that has been supporting Putin's government came under intense US scrutiny after the Russian invasion of Ukraine. In the 1990s, these politically connected businessmen, called oligarchs, were known by international law enforcement agencies to have illegally acquired extreme wealth. They have had influence over Russian policy ever since. Without their support, it is doubtful Putin would have been able to invade Ukraine. Now the United States is going after assets that the oligarchs hold most dear: their wealth.

In March 2022, the US Justice Department created Task Force KleptoCapture to sanction the oligarchs, freezing their bank accounts and seizing property. That property can include private jets, lavish mansions, and multimillion-dollar yachts. In June, the task force seized the $325 million superyacht *Amadea*, a 350-foot (106 m) vessel owned by a Russian oligarch. Officials are also in the process of confiscating two jets from an oligarch who is one of Putin's closest friends.

Some oligarchs who own assets in Western nations have spoken out against the war. But for most of Russia's richest businessmen, the future and their wealth are tied to their unwavering support of Putin.

pipeline designed to bring Russian natural gas to Germany. Completed at a cost of $11 billion, the pipeline, called Nord Stream 2, would have increased already substantial dependence on Russian energy, creating security concerns for Ukraine and EU nations. US sanctions and Germany's refusal to approve Nord Stream 2 effectively stopped the pipeline from going into service, depriving Russia of both revenue and political influence.

Unintended Consequences

One of Putin's major reasons for invading Ukraine was his unwavering demand that Ukraine never join NATO. If Ukraine chose to align with NATO, it would give Russia a 1,282-mile-long (2,063 km) border to defend. With Ukraine already seeking closer ties with the West—and memories of Cold War tensions—Putin views a stronger NATO as a threat to his ambitions for reuniting the former Soviet bloc of nations under Russia's control.

What actually happened in the wake of the Russian invasion, however, was something that Putin did not foresee. Fin-

On March 2, 2022, the members of the United Nations General Assembly, headquartered in New York City, voted on whether Russia's invasion of Ukraine should be condemned. A total of 141 nations voted to condemn; 5, including of course Russia, refused to condemn; and 35 nations abstained.

land and its neighbor to the west, Sweden, are separated from Russia by Finland's 830-mile (1,340-km) eastern border. The two nations had remained neutral for decades, preferring to provide for their own defense and not taking sides in armed conflicts between nations. That changed with Russia's 2022 invasion of Ukraine. Both countries have applied for NATO membership, a move that would provide added security in the event of a Russian attack. On June 29, NATO formally extended an offer of membership to Finland and Sweden. Although it usually takes about a year for an invited state to become a NATO member, the process will likely be accelerated due to the urgency of the war.

> "The Russian President wanted less NATO, only to end up with a lot more NATO than has existed at any time since the end of the Cold War."[43]
>
> —NATO secretary-general Jens Stoltenberg

Although Putin began his war to prevent the growth of NATO, his plan backfired. "The Russian President wanted less NATO," commented NATO's secretary-general, Jens Stoltenberg, "only to end up with a lot more NATO than has existed at any time since the end of the Cold War."[43]

Weapons for Ukraine

Although Ukraine is not a NATO member, many NATO nations and others have stepped up to help. At the outbreak of hostilities, Ukraine's military strength was far inferior to Russia's well-equipped armed forces. According to the Global Firepower website, Russia's military might ranks second in the world (behind only the United States); Ukraine ranks twenty-second. The defense budgets of the two nations are also lopsided. Russia spends about $154 billion a year on defense, whereas Ukraine's annual defense budget is $11.8 billion. In an effort to correct this gross imbalance, and improve Ukraine's chances against the Russian aggressor, many nations have given Ukraine money and military hardware.

The United States has become one of the largest benefactors of Ukraine's war effort. As of May, the United States had pledged more than $54 billion worth of security aid, including weapons

Heading Toward World War III?

One of the greatest fears to come out of the war in Ukraine is the fear that it might escalate into global nuclear war. No nation has used nuclear weapons against another since America dropped atomic bombs on Japan, ending World War II. But the specter of a nuclear holocaust has suddenly become very real.

Russia is a nuclear power. Some military experts worry that Putin may deploy tactical nuclear weapons in Ukraine. Tactical battlefield weapons are low-power nuclear missiles or bombs that have only a short-range capability. But Russia is also developing a new missile with intercontinental range. The Sarmat missile (NATO designation "Satan 2") can carry up to ten nuclear warheads a distance of 11,000 miles (18,000 km).

After Finland and Sweden announced their intention to join NATO, Aleksey Zhuravlyov, deputy chairman of Russia's parliamentary defense committee, issued a chilling warning to the West. "If the United States threatens our state, it's good: Here is the Sarmat for you, and there will be nuclear ashes from you if you think that Russia should not exist." Although Russia has had nuclear weapons for more than sixty years, it has never used them in wartime. The world is counting on that trend continuing.

Quoted in Snejana Farberov, "Putin Warns 'Satan-2' Nuclear Missiles Could Be Deployed in Months," *New York Post*, June 22, 2022. https://nypost.com.

and ammunition. But complicated logistics often creates a gap between weapons pledged and weapons delivered. For example, as of June 7, the United States had delivered about 48 percent of its pledged military equipment to Ukraine.

Among the thousands of US weapons that had been delivered were Stinger antiaircraft missiles, Javelin anti-tank missiles, armored vehicles, artillery, helicopters, UAVs or drones, and millions of rounds of ammunition. Some of the latest military technology is being sent to Ukraine, such as Switchblade UAVs, which are so-called loitering munitions that can remain in flight over an enemy area. The Switchblade can seek and destroy a target autonomously or be controlled by a ground operator who locates a suitable target via onboard video and infrared cameras. The system allows pinpoint accuracy in targeting, thus reducing damage to civilian structures and noncombatants.

Anticipating the outbreak of hostilities, the United Kingdom made its first delivery of weapons to Ukraine on January 30. After the invasion, the United Kingdom stepped up its support, sending thousands of anti-tank weapons, UAVs, missiles, and ammunition. The European Union allocated funding in the amount of $2.8 billion for military equipment to be sent to Ukraine. Rocket launchers, anti-tank weapons, armored vehicles, and electronic items such as night-vision goggles and GPS jammers are included in the EU funding.

According to the website Statista, more than 35 nations around the world have pledged assistance to Ukraine. This includes relatively small nations such as Estonia. Like Ukraine, this eastern European nation of 1.3 million people was once part of the Soviet Union. When the Soviet Union collapsed, it too declared its independence. Estonia, which considers itself to be in the path of a likely Russian expansion, has contributed $245 million to Ukraine's war effort. This represents almost 1 percent of its gross domestic product (GDP), which is a measure of a nation's wealth. America's contribution, while significantly higher, equals about 0.22 percent of US GDP.

A Ukrainian soldier unpacks some sophisticated Javelin anti-tank missiles recently shipped to Ukraine from the United States. The latter, along with other NATO nations, has also supplied Ukraine with drones, helicopters, body armor, and millions of rounds of ammunition.

In June, pledged assistance to Ukraine increased as Russian forces came closer to their goal of taking control of the Luhansk and Donetsk regions and renewed threats to target Kyiv. But some nations were slow to turn their pledges into weapons on the battlefield. Germany, for example, had delivered only one-third of its pledged military assistance to Ukraine by early June.

Ukraine's Fight for Life

The invasion of Ukraine was no surprise to the world at large: Russia's months-long military buildup along its border with Ukraine foreshadowed the conflict to come. And yet, since the invasion began, the war brought with it some unexpected circumstances. The extraordinary courage and toughness of the Ukrainian armed forces thwarted Putin's expectation of a quick victory. Despite heavy opposition, however, Russian forces destroyed much of Ukraine, reducing cities to rubble and forcing millions of Ukrainians to leave their homes in search of safety.

"We are strong. We are ready for everything. We shall win over everybody because we are Ukraine."[44]

—Ukrainian president Volodymyr Zelenskyy

Meanwhile, the world rallied around Ukraine. NATO renewed its commitment to pursue peace in Europe, and nations rich and poor contributed to Ukraine's struggle for independence. Months into the war no one could predict how much longer the fighting would last. Although Putin has tried to physically and politically destroy Ukraine, he learned early on that he could not break the spirit of the Ukrainian people and its leader. On the day after the invasion, Zelenskyy proclaimed, "We are strong. We are ready for everything. We shall win over everybody because we are Ukraine."[44]

SOURCE NOTES

Introduction: An Unprovoked Attack

1. Quoted in Bloomberg News, "Transcript: Vladimir Putin's Televised Address on Ukraine," February 24, 2022. www.bloomberg.com.
2. Quoted in Jack Guy, "'We Just Wanted to Be Together,' Says Ukrainian Couple Who Rushed to Marry Amid Attacks," CNN, February 25, 2022. www.cnn.com.

Chapter One: Russia and Ukraine: A Troubled History

3. Vladimir Putin, "Annual Address to the Federal Assembly of the Russian Federation," Presidential Executive Office, April 25, 2005. http://en.kremlin.ru.
4. Quoted in Elliott Davis Jr., "Explainer: Why Did Russia Invade Ukraine?," *U.S. News & World Report,* February 24, 2022. www.usnews.com.
5. Quoted in Olga Allenova, Elena Geda, and Vladimir Novikov, "NATO Bloc Has Broken Up into Bloc Packages," Kommersant, April 7, 2008. www.kommersant.ru.
6. Quoted in Simon Shuster, "The Freedom Fighter," *Time,* March 14, 2022. www.time.com.
7. Quoted in Andrew Higgins, "In First Meeting with Putin, Zelenskyy Plays to a Draw Despite a Bad Hand," *New York Times,* December 9, 2019. www.nytimes.com.
8. Quoted in Kyle Wilson, "Putin's NATO Power Play Stirs Disquiet Among Russia's Security Elite," *The Strategist*, January 29, 2022. www.aspistrategist.org.au.
9. Quoted in Agence France-Presse, "Putin Says Conflict in Eastern Ukraine 'Looks Like Genocide.'" *Moscow Times,* December 10, 2021. www.themoscowtimes.com.
10. Vladimir Putin, "Address by the President of the Russian Federation," Presidential Executive Office, February 21, 2022. http://en.kremlin.ru.

Chapter Two: Russia Invades Ukraine

11. Quoted in Leo Sands, "Ukraine: Kyiv Residents Spend Night Sheltering in Basements and Metro Stations," BBC News, February 25, 2022. www.bbc.com.
12. Vladimir Putin, "Address by the President of the Russian Federation," Presidential Executive Office, February 24, 2022. http://en.kremlin.ru.
13. Quoted in Valerie Hopkins, "In Video, a Defiant Zelenskyy Says, 'We Are Here,'" *New York Times,* February 25, 2022. www.nytimes.com.
14. Quoted in Shuster, "The Freedom Fighter."

15. Quoted in Sharon Braithwaite, "Zelenskyy Refuses US Offer to Evacuate, Saying 'I Need Ammunition, Not a Ride,'" CNN, February 26, 2022. www.cnn.com.
16. Quoted in Patrick J. McDonnell, "Russia Lost the Battle for Kyiv with Its Hasty Assault on a Ukrainian Airport," *San Diego Union-Tribune,* April 11, 2022. www.sandiegouniontribune.com.
17. Quoted in Valerie Hopkins, Ivan Nechepurenko, and Marc Santora, "The Ukrainian Authorities Declare an End to the Combat Mission in Mariupol After Weeks of Russian Siege," *New York Times,* May 16, 2022. www.nytimes.com.
18. Quoted in Greg Norman, "Ukraine-Russian War: UK Video Shows Moscow's 'Costly Failure,'" Fox News, June 3, 2022. www.foxnews.com.
19. Quoted in Siobhán O'Grady, Anastacia Galouchka, and Paul Sonne, "'They're in Hell': Hail of Russian Artillery Tests Ukrainian Morale," *Washington Post,* June 3, 2022. www.washingtonpost.com.
20. Quoted in Ishaan Tharoor, "Russian Advances in Ukraine's East Mark a Tipping Point," *Washington Post,* May 31, 2022. www.washingtonpost.com.
21. Quoted in Philissa Cramer, "18 Things to Know About Volodymyr Zelenskyy, Showman, 'Paddington' Voice and Jewish Defender of Ukrainian Democracy," Jewish Telegraphic Agency, March 1, 2022. www.jta.org.

Chapter Three: Ukraine Fights Back

22. Quoted in John Bolger, "In Ukraine's West, Conscripts of All Ages Head to Battle, Expressing Outrage at Putin's Invasion," The Intercept, February 26, 2022. www.theintercept.com.
23. Quoted in Volodymyr Zelenskyy, "Address by the President to Ukrainians at the End of the First Day of Russia's Attacks," Office of the President of Ukraine, February 25, 2022. www.president.gov.ua.
24. Quoted in Sinéad Baker, "Zelenskyy Says Ukraine Is Losing 60 to 100 Soldiers a Day, a Rare Glimpse of Ukraine's Losses During Russia's Invasion," Insider, June 1, 2022. www.businessinsider.com.
25. Quoted in Akbar Shahid Ahmed, "'Ordinary People, Extraordinary Things': Civilian Resistance Is Key to Ukraine's Defense," *World News* (blog), HuffPost, April 7, 2022. www.huffpost.com.
26. Quoted in Yarden Michaeli and Tomer Appelbaum, "Molotov Cocktails for Freedom: Ukrainians Behind the Front Lines Join the War Against Russia," *Haaretz*, March 1, 2022. www.haaretz.com.
27. Quoted in Luke Harding, "'I Haven't Told My Granny': Ukraine's Student Molotov Cocktail–Makers," *The Guardian,* February 28, 2022. www.theguardian.com.
28. Quoted in Mia Jankowicz, "Hackers Replaced Russian TV Schedules During Putin's 'Victory Day' Parade with Anti-War Messages, Saying the Blood of Ukrainians Is on Russians' Hands," Insider, May 9, 2022. www.businessinsider.com.
29. Aerorozvidka, "About Us." www.aerorozvidka.xyz.

30. Quoted in Julian Borger, "The Drone Operators Who Halted Russian Convoy Headed for Kyiv," *The Guardian,* March 28, 2022. www.theguardian.com.

31. Maciej Bartkowski, "Ukrainians vs. Putin: Potential for Nonviolent Civilian-Based Defense," *Minds of the Moment* (blog), International Center for Nonviolent Conflict, December 27, 2021. www.nonviolentconflict.org.

Chapter Four: Humanitarian Tragedies of the War

32. Quoted in CBS News, "Refugees by Rail: Ukrainians Flee War at Home," *60 Minutes,* March 6, 2022. www.cbs.com.

33. Quoted in Andres Schipani, "Millions of Ukrainians Seek Safety Within War-Torn Country's Borders," *Financial Times,* March 25, 2022. www.ft.com.

34. Quoted in Igor Kossov, "Uncovering the Scope of the Bucha Massacre," *Kyiv Independent*, April 22, 2022. www.kyivindependent.com.

35. Quoted in Tara John, Jonny Hallam, and Nathan Hodge, "Bodies of 'Executed People' Strewn Across Street in Bucha as Ukraine Accuses Russia of War Crimes," CNN, April 3, 2022. www.cnn.com.

36. Quoted in Carlotta Gall, "Bucha: The Epicenter of Russian Atrocity," in "Death in Ukraine: A Special Report," *New York Times,* June 18, 2022. www.nytimes.com.

37. Joseph R. Biden, "Remarks by President Biden After Marine One Arrival," White House, April 4, 2022. www.whitehouse.gov.

38. Wolfgang Benedek, Veronika Bílková, and Marco Sassòli, "Report on Violations of International Humanitarian and Human Rights Law, War Crimes and Crimes Against Humanity Committed in Ukraine Since 24 February 2022," Organization for Security and Co-Operation in Europe, April 13, 2022. www.osce.org.

39. Quoted in Luke Hardin and Shaun Walker, "Russia Accused of 'Monstrous' War Crime in Kramatorsk Station Attack," *The Guardian,* April 9, 2022. www.theguardian.com.

Chapter Five: The World Reacts

40. Joseph R. Biden, "Remarks by President Biden Announcing Response to Russian Actions in Ukraine," White House, February 22, 2022. www.whitehouse.gov.

41. Quoted in Robin Pomeroy, "What Are Sanctions, and Are We in a New Era of Economic War?," World Economic Forum, April 8, 2022. www.weforum.org.

42. Quoted in Chad de Guzman and Eloise Barry, "'There Is No Purgatory for War Criminals.' World Condemns Russian Invasion of Ukraine," *Time,* February 24, 2022. www.time.com.

43. Quoted in Suchet Vir Singh and Raghav Bikhchandani, "US, UK & Europe Have Sent Ukraine Weapons Worth Billions. Their Post-War Fate Is Stoking Worry," The Print, June 7, 2022. https://theprint.in.

44. Quoted in Jeremy Herb, Donald Judd, and Phil Mattingly, "Biden Condemns 'Russia's Unprovoked and Unjustified Attack on Ukraine,'" CNN, February 4, 2022. www.cnn.com.

ORGANIZATIONS AND WEBSITES

Flashpoint Ukraine
www.voanews.com
This Voice of America website is dedicated to its radio program *Flashpoint Ukraine*. The program features daily episodes on the war in Ukraine and numerous videos illuminating various aspects of the conflict.

International Committee of the Red Cross (ICRC)
www.icrc.org
The ICRC is an independent organization that promotes humanitarian protection and assistance for victims of armed conflict. Its website contains videos explaining the rules of war and humanitarian law, a section devoted to the Russia-Ukraine war, and a list of frequently asked questions about international humanitarian law.

North Atlantic Treaty Organization (NATO)
www.nato.int
NATO is an alliance of thirty nations in Europe and North America pledged to foster peace throughout Europe. The website includes an online multimedia experience with information about NATO's mission and structure; an interactive map; videos, documents, and posters about NATO's history; and details about its student internship program.

Office of the High Commissioner for Human Rights (OHCHR)
www.ohchr.org
The OHCHR is the agency of the United Nations responsible for promoting and protecting human rights around the world. This site includes articles on human rights as they pertain to justice, nondiscrimination, business practices, the environment, and human dignity.

Official Website of Ukraine
https://ukraine/ua
Visitors to this website can choose to see a section on the war or look at Ukraine before the hostilities began. These sections feature photographs, videos, articles, and more about Ukraine, both at peace and as a nation coping with the horrors of war.

"Vladimir Putin: Russia's Action Man President"
www.bbc.com
This website traces the life of Vladimir Putin from birth to the invasion of Ukraine. It provides insight into the man who rules Russia with an iron fist and includes photographs, a chronology of his life, and links to other articles about him.

Books

Paul D'Anieri, *Ukraine and Russia: From Civilized Divorce to Uncivil War*. Cambridge, UK: Cambridge University Press, 2019.

Serhii Plokhy, *The Gates of Europe: A History of Ukraine*. New York: Basic Books, 2021.

Vladimir Putin, *First Person: An Astonishingly Frank Self-Portrait by Russia's President Vladimir Putin*. New York: Public Affairs, 2000.

Erik Richardson, *NATO, the Warsaw Pact, and the Iron Curtain.* New York: Cavendish Square, 2018.

Serhy Yekelchyk, *Ukraine: What Everyone Needs to Know*. New York: Oxford University Press, 2020.

Internet Sources

Luke Harding, "'I Haven't Told My Granny': Ukraine's Student Molotov Cocktail–Makers," *The Guardian*, February 28, 2022. www.theguardian.com.

Daniel Hunter, "How Ukrainian Civilians Are Resisting Military Force," *Yes!,* March 1, 2022. www.yesmagazine.org.

Shany Littman, translated by Olena Trofimchuk, "'We Packed Fast': Those Who Left Ukraine, in Their Own Words," *Financial Times*, March 31, 2022. www.ft.com.

Pranshu Verma, "How the 3D-Printing Community Worldwide Is Aiding Ukraine." *Washington Post*, June 12, 2022. www.washingtonpost.com.

Visual Journalism Team, "Ukraine War in Maps: Tracking the Russian Invasion," BBC News, July 4, 2022. www.bbc.com.